★ FACTS AMERICA

OUR NATIONAL
PARKS

ROBIN & POLLY MEAD AND ANDREW GUTELLE

SMITHMARK

About the authors

Robin Mead is an author and journalist whose work appears in newspapers and magazines around the world. An avid traveler, Mr. Mead has written numerous books and travel guides. His wife, Polly Mead, trained as a teacher and worked in the travel industry before joining her husband as full-time co-writer, researcher, and "organizer in chief."

Andrew Gutelle is a children's author with a strong interest in science and nature. He is a writer for the Emmy Award-winning television series "Reading Rainbow." Mr. Gutelle also created *3-2-1 Contact* magazine, winner of a National Magazine Award for Excellence. He is a member of the Writers' Guild of America and the Society of Children's Book Writers.

Editor:
Philip de Ste. Croix

Designer:
Stonecastle Graphics Ltd

Picture research:
Leora Kahn

Coordinating editors:
Andrew Preston
Kristen Schilo

Production:
Ruth Arthur
Sally Connolly
Neil Randles
Andrew Whitelaw

Production editor:
Didi Charney

Director of production:
Gerald Hughes

Typesetter:
Pagesetters Incorporated

Color and monochrome reproduction:
Advance Laser Graphic Arts, Hong Kong

Printed and bound in Hong Kong by
Leefung-Asco Printers Ltd

1992 Colour Library Books Ltd
Godalming Business Centre
Woolsack Way, Godalming
Surrey GU7 1XW, United Kingdom
CLB 2607

This edition published in 1992 by
SMITHMARK Publishers Inc.
112 Madison Avenue
New York, NY 10016 USA

SMITHMARK books are available for bulk purchase for sales promotion and premium use. For details, write or call the manager of special sales, SMITHMARK Publishers Inc., 112 Madison Avenue, New York, NY 10016; (212) 532-6600.

Library of Congress Cataloging-in-Publication Data

Mead, Robin.
    Facts America. Our national parks / Robin & Polly Mead & Andrew Gutelle.
        p.   cm.
    Includes bibliographical references and index.
    Summary: Discusses the sights and activities of over thirty national parks.
    ISBN 0-8317-2314-9 (hardcover)
    1. National parks and reserves—United States—Juvenile literature. [1. National parks and reserves.]   I. Mead, Polly, 1946–   II. Gutelle, Andrew.   III. Title.   IV. Title: Our national parks.
E160.M36   1992
917.302—dc20   92-9460

This tranquil scene can be found in Colorado's Rocky Mountain National Park. In the foreground is the poetically named Dream Lake; over it towers majestic Flattop Mountain. It is easy to see how it was named!

Contents

Introduction

From coast to coast and beyond, the United States includes places of incredible natural beauty. Many of America's most spectacular sights are found in its national parks. These public lands are part of our country's national park system. The United States was the first country in the world to preserve land for its people in this fashion.

Today, there are 49 national parks in the United States. There are more than 300 other places that are also protected in the national park system. Many of these parklands recognize landmarks and sites of historic importance. Others have been set aside for wildlife preservation or for recreation. Nearly all of these places are the responsibility of the National Park Service.

YELLOWSTONE IS FIRST: The national park movement began in the mid-1800s. As people explored the West, they brought back stories of amazing sights. One unbelievable tale told of underground springs shooting water hundreds of feet into the air. These geysers were said to exist in the Yellowstone region of the Rocky Mountains. In 1869, the government sent a scientific expedition to investigate this rumor. One year later, a team of surveyors followed. They discovered that the bubbling hot springs and geysers did exist.

When the men returned from their adventure, they put forward a unique idea. Instead of

▲ This map shows the current extent of our country's national park system. In addition to these parks, historical monuments, and landmarks, wildlife preserves and recreational areas are also part of the system. Every state except Delaware has some preserved land.

◄ Sunlight shows the rich color of Bryce Canyon National Park. As Americans moved west, they discovered beautiful views and magnificent scenery. This helped create interest in saving land for future generations.

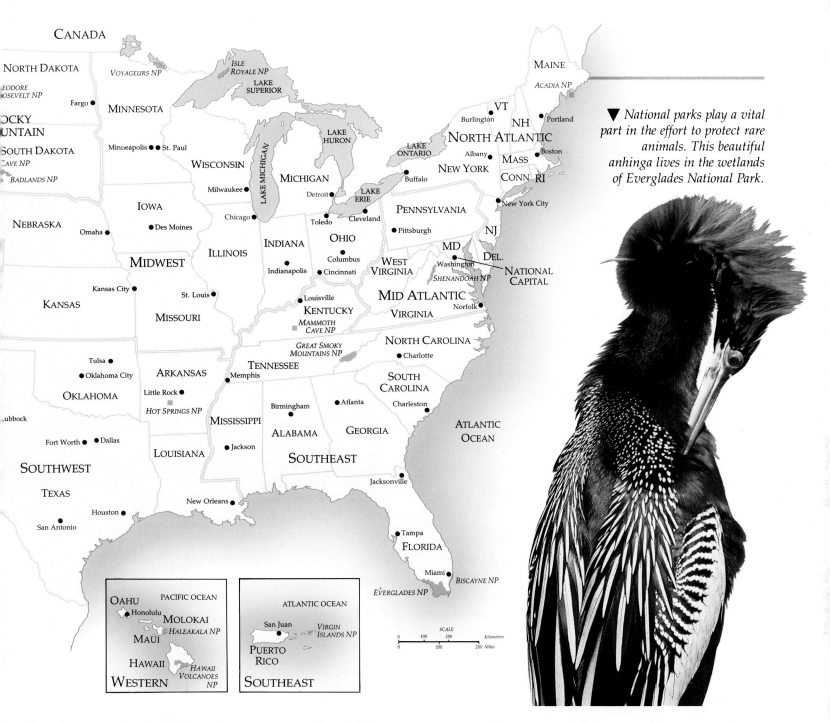

NORTH DAKOTA

VOYAGEURS NP

ISLE ROYALE NP

LAKE SUPERIOR

MAINE

ACADIA NP

EODORE OSEVELT NP

Fargo •

MINNESOTA

▼ *National parks play a vital part in the effort to protect rare animals. This beautiful anhinga lives in the wetlands of Everglades National Park.*

OCKY UNTAIN

Minneapolis • • St. Paul

LAKE HURON

VT

Burlington • NH

• Portland

SOUTH DAKOTA

WISCONSIN

LAKE ONTARIO

NORTH ATLANTIC

CAVE NP

Milwaukee •

MICHIGAN

Albany • MASS • Boston

• Buffalo

NEW YORK CONN RI

BADLANDS NP

Detroit •

LAKE ERIE

IOWA

Chicago •

LAKE MICHIGAN

• New York City

NEBRASKA

Des Moines •

PENNSYLVANIA

NJ

Omaha •

ILLINOIS

INDIANA

OHIO

Columbus •

Toledo • • Cleveland

• Pittsburgh

MD

MIDWEST

Indianapolis • • Cincinnati

WEST VIRGINIA

Washington • DEL.

SHENANDOAH NP NATIONAL CAPITAL

KANSAS

Kansas City •

St. Louis •

Louisville •

MID ATLANTIC

Norfolk •

MISSOURI

KENTUCKY

VIRGINIA

MAMMOTH CAVE NP

NORTH CAROLINA

Tulsa •

GREAT SMOKY MOUNTAINS NP

• Charlotte

• Oklahoma City

ARKANSAS

TENNESSEE

OKLAHOMA

Little Rock •

Memphis •

SOUTH CAROLINA

Charleston •

HOT SPRINGS NP

Birmingham •

• Atlanta

Lubbock

MISSISSIPPI

• Dallas

ALABAMA

GEORGIA

ATLANTIC OCEAN

Fort Worth •

LOUISIANA

• Jackson

SOUTHWEST

SOUTHEAST

TEXAS

Houston •

New Orleans •

Jacksonville •

San Antonio •

• Tampa

FLORIDA

Miami • *BISCAYNE NP*

EVERGLADES NP

OAHU PACIFIC OCEAN

Honolulu • MOLOKAI

HALEAKALA NP

MAUI

HAWAII

HAWAII VOLCANOES NP

WESTERN

ATLANTIC OCEAN

San Juan

VIRGIN ISLANDS NP

PUERTO RICO

SOUTHEAST

SCALE

0   100   200   Kilometers

0   100   200 Miles

dividing up the land for private use, it should be preserved for everyone. In 1872, Yellowstone became the world's first national park.

The park system grew slowly. By 1916, there were 11 parks and 18 national monuments. The U.S. Congress realized that the parks needed to be carefully managed. An agency was established to run the parks. The people of the National Park Service had two responsibilities. They would preserve America's parklands in their natural condition. They would also make parks accessible to visitors who wanted to see them.

POPULARITY BRINGS PROBLEMS: Today, there are 80 million acres of parkland in the national park

system—about as much area as the state of New Mexico. Millions of people visit them every year. Many stay in lodges and campgrounds in the parks themselves. In recent years, the National Park Service has struggled hard to prevent overcrowding. Overuse, and the pollution it brings, is a constant problem.

People share these beautiful lands with plants and animals that rely on the parks for survival. Because national parks and preserves have been kept undisturbed, they provide safe homes for many endangered species. Like the parks themselves, these plants and animals are a part of our country's past that must be preserved for future generations.

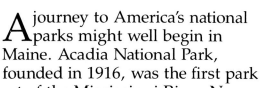

The East *Acadia*

A journey to America's national parks might well begin in Maine. Acadia National Park, founded in 1916, was the first park established east of the Mississippi River. New England is filled with monuments and landmarks, but Acadia is its only national park.

Acadia is a small park. Most of its 40,000 acres are located on Mount Desert Island. In spite of its name, the rocky island is hardly barren. In the spring, it is covered with more than 500 varieties of wildflowers. In the fall, the maple trees display their brilliant red and orange colors.

A RETREAT FOR THE WEALTHY: In the late 1900s, Acadia's beauty attracted wealthy Americans like John D. Rockefeller. They constructed summer homes on the island. Rockefeller also built a network of gravel paths and stone bridges. These roads allowed people to explore the island on foot or by horse-drawn carriage. Eventually, Rockefeller donated 11,000 acres to the national park system.

Visitors to Acadia still walk Rockefeller's footpaths. They climb Cadillac Mountain and enjoy fabulous views of the Atlantic Ocean. Bird-watchers can look for more than 275 species of birds that live in the park at various times of year.

▼ *The lighthouse at Bass Harbor shines above Mount Desert Island's rocky coastline. At the southern tip of Acadia, it has been in operation since 1858.*

▼ *Gravel paths and footbridges provide the best view of Acadia's scenery. There are over 150 miles of pathways winding through the national park. In the summer months, guides lead visitors over its rocky trails.*

Shenandoah

▲ *The Shenandoah Valley sits below the Blue Ridge Mountains. It was Native Americans who named the region Shenandoah, which means "daughter of the stars."*

▼ *Mount Desert Island's landscape was carved by glaciers thousands of years ago. Smooth, polished boulders are a product of its glacial past.*

Shenandoah National Park is bordered by the Blue Ridge Mountains on one side and the Shenandoah River on the other. It is located in Virginia, about 75 miles from Washington, D.C. Surrounded by a densely populated area, the park's 195,000 acres are almost entirely forest. Much of the park looks the way it did before the first European settlers arrived.

Shenandoah became a national park in 1926. At the time, most of the land was owned by private citizens. Much of this property had been used as farms or pastureland. It took the state of Virginia ten years to acquire nearly 4,000 tracts of land. Since the park opened, the land has slowly returned to its natural state.

DRIVING THE SKYLINE: Running along the crest of the Blue Ridge Mountains is one of the most scenic roads in America. Skyline Drive travels 105 miles through the park. Views from the highway are spectacular. Shenandoah also provides for travel on foot. There are over 500 miles of hiking paths. The Appalachian Trail winds for 96 miles through the park.

Mammoth Cave

Hidden beneath the southern Kentucky countryside is the largest known system of caves in the world. Mammoth Cave National Park is a series of tunnels and caverns. About 330 miles of cave have been explored so far.

Mammoth Cave is located halfway between Louisville, Kentucky, and Nashville, Tennessee. This area is called the Southern Sinkhole Plain. Beneath the ground is a thick layer of sandstone. Below that is limestone. When rainwater sinks through holes in the sandstone, it reaches the limestone. Over time, flowing water has carved out incredible cave formations.

SHAKESPEARE AND SNOWBALLS: Visitors can explore about 12 miles of Mammoth Cave. Guided tours lead to many of the cave's best-known formations. Frozen Niagara is a 75-foot-high display of flowstone. These startling columns of limestone were built over thousands of years by dripping water. Booth's Amphitheater is a huge chamber. It is named for the actor Edwin Booth, who once recited Shakespeare there. In the Snowball Room, clusters of the mineral gypsum appear frozen to the ceiling.

A hiker explores Mammoth Cave. Overhead is a typical cave formation. The featherlike pattern was slowly carved by water dripping from above.

▲ *Parts of the Great Smokies receive more than 100 inches of rain. Not surprisingly, there are 600 miles of streams in the park. There are also many waterfalls, including Grotto Falls seen here.*

Great Smoky Mountains

▼ *The Great Smokies are almost always shrouded in haze and mist. Some of the best views are from the Blue Ridge Parkway, which runs through the center of the national park.*

▲ *A curtain of ice covers a rock formation in the Great Smokies. Snowfall is a regular winter event here, although spring weather sometimes arrives as early as January.*

On the border of Tennessee and North Carolina is Great Smoky Mountains National Park. The park covers half a million acres and includes some of the oldest mountains on earth.

The Great Smokies are the tallest mountains in the eastern United States. There are 25 peaks that are more than 6,000 feet high. The mountains are named for the smokelike haze that covers their highest peaks and ridges.

The Cherokee people lived in the Great Smokies for hundreds of years. European settlers arrived after the American Revolution. By the time plans were announced to form a national park in 1926, timber companies owned 85 percent of the land. As in Shenandoah, the government raised money to purchase the land from the timber companies and farmers who owned it.

FORESTS, MEADOWS, AND MORE: Visitors are drawn to this national park by its lush beauty. The moist climate provides a perfect environment for plant growth. Its forests include over 1,300 varieties of trees and shrubs. At the edges of the forest are meadows covered with flowering plants. The abandoned cabins, farms, and churches of early settlers are also popular attractions.

Everglades

The first great national parks protected beautiful or unusual scenery. Everglades National Park was established in 1947 for a different reason. This vast park was formed to protect a fragile ecosystem.

Everglades includes 1.4 million acres of wetland in south Florida. At first glance, the park seems flat and uninteresting. A closer look reveals swaying seas of grass, dense clumps of tropical undergrowth, and forests rising from its swamps.

This unique land is home to an incredible variety of wildlife. Hundreds of kinds of rare birds live there, including herons, egrets, brown pelicans, and bald eagles. The Everglades's shallow waters provide homes for alligators, green sea turtles, and sea cows, called manatees. Land animals including the Florida panther, black bear, deer, and bobcat also live there.

The Everglades is home to over 300 species of birds. The beautiful anhinga often perches in tall grass and trees. The bird feeds on fish, which it spears with its pointed bill.

THE STRUGGLE FOR WATER: The most important ingredient in the Everglades's mix of plant and animal life is water. The wetlands are fed by water flowing from the Big Cypress Swamp and Lake Okeechobee to the north. In the past, development of Cypress and Okeechobee created problems for the Everglades. Dikes and drainage ditches prevented the natural flow of water. The lack of water changed the delicate balance of nature in the region. It also increased the chance for damaging fires during the dry season.

▲ *Although the Everglades is mostly a sea of grass, tree islands, called hammocks, are a common sight. Tree roots take hold in limestone or in muck that has collected to form dry land.*

A grove of cypress trees ▶ reaches to the sky. Cypress and pine forests grow in the swampy regions of the Everglades.

◀ *The most famous native of the Everglades is the American alligator. Once endangered, the reptile is protected in this habitat.*

The Everglades is a delicate ▶ blend of water and vegetation. The highest point in the national park is only seven feet above sea level.

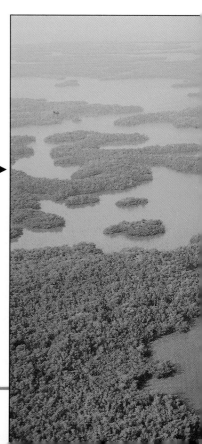

In recent years, officials have taken steps to protect the park. The Big Cypress National Preserve prevents the swamp to the north from further development. Officials hope to purchase wetlands east of the park to push development away from its edges.

A POPULAR PARK: Because it is only 30 miles from Miami, many people visit the Everglades. Airboats skim over the shallow water and provide safe views of the habitat. Some visitors rent canoes and wind their way through the park at a slower pace. Boardwalks allow for short hikes above the murky water. A walk on the boards of the Anhinga Trail reveals alligators, water snakes, and wading birds in the water below.

Biscayne

South of the tip of Florida lies a string of islands, called keys. Between Key Biscayne and Key Largo is Biscayne Bay. This unusual national park is almost entirely underwater.

The most spectacular sights at Biscayne are its underwater coral reefs. Created by tiny animals called polyps, the reefs have been built up over many centuries. Some coral reefs rise hundreds of feet from the ocean floor. The reefs run for 150 miles along the Florida Keys.

BOATING AND DIVING: Visitors ride in glass-bottom boats to see the network of coral in Biscayne. Snorkelers and scuba divers plunge into the warm water for a closer look at the reefs. Living there are hundreds of kinds of unusual and colorful sea creatures, including porcupine fish, parrot fish, angelfish, starfish, and sea anemones.

Biscayne was established to prevent overdevelopment of the land in south Florida. When it became a national landmark in 1968, the bay and the thickets of mangrove trees at its shore were included. In 1980, the protected region was greatly expanded and the bay became a national park.

▼ *The Cape Florida lighthouse on Key Biscayne is the northern boundary of the bay. For centuries, coral reefs hidden in shallow waters have caused many shipwrecks. Scuba divers visit the remains of some wrecks on the reefs.*

Virgin Islands

▲ *Mangrove trees line the shore of Biscayne National Park. Their tangled roots protect birds and fish from land animals. The roots also guard against erosion.*

▼ *Plants hug the rocky shore of Salt Pond Bay on St. John. The Caribbean island is home to 800 species of plants.*

▲ *Many of St. John's treasures can be seen beneath the clear waters that surround the island. Coral reefs are home to tropical fish and other sea creatures.*

Not all national parks are located in the 50 states. Virgin Islands National Park is found on the Caribbean island of St. John. The entire island, and the water around it, is protected parkland.

The Virgin Islands were visited by Christopher Columbus during his second voyage to America. In the following years, the islands became a popular base for pirates who sailed the Caribbean Sea. In the 1700s, Danish settlers built sugar plantations and brought slave labor to the islands. Finally, in 1917, the islands were purchased by the United States.

AN ISLAND PARADISE: Warm tropical weather and cool breezes make St. John a popular vacation spot. The island is covered with thick tropical forests and beautiful white sand beaches. Like Biscayne, the greatest attractions at this national park lie below the water. Surrounding the island are 5,000 acres of coral reefs.

One of the best snorkling spots is just off beautiful Trunk Bay Beach. An underwater nature trail allows snorkelers to follow a path along a coral reef. As they swim the trail, they see signs etched on glass, which explain how the reefs were formed. Also described are the beautiful sea creatures waiting to be discovered.

2 *Mid-America* *Isle Royale*

Isle Royale is a wild, undeveloped national park in Michigan. The park is located on one main island and 200 smaller ones in Lake Superior. The surrounding water has protected this wilderness for hundreds of years.

Isle Royale's parkland is a natural preserve. Most animals must swim or fly to reach it. Animals living there include beavers, muskrats, snowshoe hares, and red foxes. During severe winters, moose and wolves walked across Lake Superior's ice to settle there.

A NATURAL LABORATORY: Scientists are particularly interested in the wildlife on Isle Royale. For decades, they have studied the relationship of the moose herd and wolf pack on the island. Wolves feed on old, young, and weak moose. They keep the herd size from growing too large for the island. Neither wolves or moose could survive on Isle Royale without each other.

People have a long history on Isle Royale, too. Ancient copper pits have been discovered on the island. These suggest people came there 4,500 years ago. Visitors still come today. They arrive by boat or seaplane to hike the trails of one of America's wildest national parks.

▼ Moose antlers blend into Isle Royale's undergrowth. The first moose walked across frozen Lake Superior to get here.

Voyageurs

◀ A mist conceals the delights that await visitors to Isle Royale. Hidden in the national park's half-million acres is a rich variety of plant and animal life.

Glaciers once carved their ▶ way along Voyageur's Kabetogama Peninsula. The smooth rocks left along the shore provide sights for camping or picnicki...

▼ The colors of s... Isle Royale's ... ago, a de... hardw... tree... ri...

At the northern border of Minnesota is a wilderness of lakes, streams, woods, and swamps, called Voyageurs National Park. It is named for the French-Canadian trappers and traders who canoed these waterways. Many carried furs from northwest Canada back to Montreal.

Most of Voyageurs is located on the heavily forested Kabetogama Peninsula of Minnesota. About a third of the park's 218,000 acres are underwater. There are more than 100 lakes there. The old trail of lakes and streams running through the park creates part of the border between the United States and Canada.

WILD RICE AND CRANBERRIES: Voyageurs has always been a remote wilderness. Native Americans once lived on these waters. The Sioux and the Chippewa came in birch-bark canoes to hunt and fish. They harvested cranberries from its bogs and wild rice from shallow bays and streams.

Today, people still explore the park in canoes. Many of the campsites can only be reached by boat. Once there, visitors walk narrow footpaths to many beautiful lakes hidden in the peninsula's forest.

Hot Springs

In many ways, Hot Springs is unique. Its 5,800 acres make it America's smallest national park. It was set aside as a federal reserve in 1832—40 years before Yellowstone became the first national park.

The attraction at Hot Springs is the 47 pools of warm water that bubble up naturally from the ground. Nearly one million gallons of water fill the springs every day. The water at Hot Springs was long believed to be a cure for many medical problems.

BATHHOUSES FOR THE RICH: Hot Springs is not parkland preserved in its natural state. In the 1800s, a beautiful resort town for the wealthy was built there. Today, the elegant buildings of Central Avenue are the core of the national park. This street is also called Bathhouse Row.

On Bathhouse Row, the Buckstaff still offers visitors the chance to take a relaxing bath in naturally heated spring water. Another popular stop is the Fordyce. This bathhouse has been carefully restored. Visitors there see what a trip to the spa was like more than a century ago.

▲ *The resort town at Hot Springs was built in the 1800s. It was made to look like the stylish resorts, called spas, that were popular in Europe.*

The Rio Grande winds for ▶ 107 miles along the border of Big Bend. The towering Chisos Mountains border the park to the north.

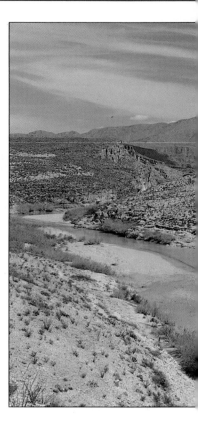

▶ *The mineral water at Hot Springs is naturally heated to 143° F. The blue-green water is colored by tiny plants, called algae.*

▼ *Bathhouse Row is the center of Hot Springs. Most of the bathhouses are no longer in operation. Daily tours begin at the Health Services Bathhouse.*

Meteor Shower
FUN FACTS

Meteor showers
are named for the
constellation they
appear to be coming
from in the sky.

Meteor Shower
FUN FACTS

A meteor is the streak of light we see in the sky from a meteoroid, or space rock. A meteorite is a space rock that hits the surface of Earth.

When Earth moves through the trails of dust and rock left behind by comets or asteroids we see a meteor shower. The streaks of light we see are made by the glowing hot air surrounding the meteoroid.

Most meteorites fall into the ocean. Rarely, they fall on land and are found by people.

Every day, millions of meteoroids pass through Earth's atmosphere.

There are 21 meteor showers throughout the year. These include the Perseids, the Geminids, the Leonids, and the Lyrids.

During the Perseids and Geminids, skywatchers might see 50 – 100 meteors per hour.

▲ *For many years, the rough land of Big Bend kept people from exploring it. Today, more than 350 miles of trails lead visitors to its natural treasures.*

As the Rio Grande winds along the Texas border, it makes a giant U-shaped curve. This is Big Bend. The national park's 800,000 acres include the Rio Grande, huge desert plains, and the Chisos Mountains.

The sights at Big Bend are spectacular. The Rio Grande has carved three beautiful canyons, including St. Elena. This chasm is so deep that at times, sunlight does not reach the bottom. To the north, the Chisos Mountains rise above the desert plain. The craggy peaks named Casa Grande and Emory are more than 7,800 feet high.

CAMELS AND CRIMINALS: Big Bend has an odd and fascinating history. In 1859, the army brought camels to this desert. They hoped to train them for use in the American Southwest. Later, the rough terrain of Big Bend became a hideout for train robbers and bandits.

The rugged land was unmapped until 1899. Since then, many discoveries have been made. Fossils of dinosaurs and other prehistoric creatures have been found. Traces of ancient civilizations have also been uncovered.

Big Bend may look barren, but it is teeming with life. There are more than 1,000 species of plants and 400 varieties of birds. Mountain lions, pronghorn antelope, and coyotes live there, too.

For centuries, people wandering the west Texas desert have seen El Capitan. This peak of the Guadalupe Mountains rises above the desert plains. It is the center of Guadalupe Mountains National Park.

The Guadalupe Mountains run along the border of Texas and New Mexico. The mountains are made of ancient land. Fossils show this was an ocean reef that formed 250 million years ago. Over time, the water dried up and the reef was buried. About 12 million years ago, forces in the earth pushed up a portion of the reef to form the 40-mile-long mountain range.

ANCIENT TREASURES: Archaeologists have found spear tips, knife blades, and bits of pottery used by people more than 12,000 years ago. In more recent times, Spanish explorers and Mescalero Apaches camped here. In the 1800s, prospectors, ranchers, and farmers followed.

Today, McKittrick Canyon is popular with visitors. The canyon's streams are fed by underground springs. Its walls are lined with maple, oak, and cottonwood trees. According to legend, bank robber Kit McKittrick's loot is still buried somewhere in the canyon.

▲ *The Guadalupe Mountains are a V-shaped range. El Capitan and Guadalupe Peak are at its midpoint. They are the tallest peaks in Texas.*

▼ *El Capitan can been seen from 50 miles away. Its Spanish name means "the chief."*

The ancient reef that formed the Guadalupe Mountains worked its wonder beneath the ground, too. Just over the border to the north lies New Mexico's Carlsbad Caverns National Park. Its 20 miles of explored tunnels and chambers feature some of the most stunning cave sights in the world.

Carlsbad is home of Mexican free-tailed bat. Every night, half a million bats swarm out of the cave. They feed on insects and return at dawn. People discovered the caverns by following the cloud of bats. For many years, they mined the caves. The bats' waste, called guano, was collected and used as fertilizer.

BOGGLING SIGHTS BELOW: Visitors enter the cave and follow a trail that descends 830 feet into the earth. The limestone formations are varied and enormous. Largest of all is the Big Room. It is as wide as 12 football fields. It is nearly tall enough to fit the Statue of Liberty standing inside it! Other cavern wonders have fanciful names that describe a magical hidden world. These include Fairyland, Mirror Lake, Iceberg Rock, and the Boneyard.

▲ *There are 70 chambers inside Carlsbad Caverns. Stalactites and stalagmites are common sights. Many rooms have been carefully lit, adding to their eerie beauty.*

▼ *A natural opening leads into Carlsbad. The entrance provides access for people during the day and for hundreds of thousands of bats at night.*

3 The Rockies *Theodore Roosevelt*

Theodore Roosevelt was one of the first presidents to champion the cause of conservation. He set aside millions of acres for preservation. Theodore Roosevelt National Park honors his commitment to this cause.

Roosevelt arrived in the wild Dakota Territory in 1883. He came to hunt buffalo, which were nearly extinct. Roosevelt fell in love with this untamed country. Two years later, he bought the Maltese Cross Ranch and became a rancher. Soon after, he bought a second ranch—the Elkhorn.

Like many before him, Roosevelt discovered how hard prairie life could be. In 1887, a severe winter wiped out his herd. He returned to the East. However, Roosevelt never forgot his experience in the Dakotas or his love for the wild land he had found there.

BEAUTIFUL BADLANDS: Theodore Roosevelt National Park is in North Dakota. Its 70,000 acres run along the Little Missouri River. The park is a blend of prairie and the rugged terrain, known as badlands. Herd animals thrive on its grassy plains. Buffalo, mule deer, pronghorn antelope, and wild horses live there.

The parkland is divided into two sections that lie 60 miles apart. The historical south unit includes portions of Roosevelt's ranch. His home at Maltese Cross has been moved and restored. The north unit of the park is wilder and more scenic. Visitors there get a glimpse of the world Roosevelt saw over 100 years ago.

◀ *Much of Theodore Roosevelt National Park is badlands. Erosion wears the rocky land into odd and intriguing shapes.*

Throughout the park, ▶ *overlooks provide views of badlands. They reveal layers of rock and little vegetation. Much of the work of carving this land was done by the Little Missouri River.*

▼ *The park's grassy plains are similar to the African savanna. Ranchers once raised cattle on this land. Today, animals like buffalo have reclaimed it.*

A hiker enjoys the sunset ▶ *in Wind Cave National Park. The caverns beneath his feet are filled with crystal formations.*

Wind Cave

Near Mount Rushmore and South Dakota's Black Hills is a small patch of preserved prairie. The 28,000 acres of Wind Cave National Park are home to buffalo and antelope. But, as the park's name suggests, there is more to be seen there. Lying beneath the grassland is a fascinating network of caverns.

Wind Cave was probably known to the Sioux tribe. In 1881, a Black Hills settler named Tom Bingham discovered it while hunting antelope. According to the story, a wind gusting from a hole in the prairie blew the hat off his head. Tom and his brother, Jesse, brought people to see the cave. In 1903, Wind Cave became the first cavern added to the national park system.

A DRY, DELICATE CAVERN: Wind Cave is carved from limestone but is dryer than Mammoth Cave or Carlsbad Caverns. Few large structures like stalactites and stalagmites formed there. Instead, visitors discover delicate patterns in pink and white. Wind Cave is most famous for its fine crystal designs, called boxwork.

▼ *Once 60 million buffalo roamed the prairie. In the 1880s, they were hunted to near extinction.*

Today, herds live protected lives on prairie parklands.

Badlands

Hidden in the Great Plains of South Dakota is a land of dazzling rock formations. At the edge of the grassland, a wall of rock forms towers and twisting pinnacles, like a giant natural castle. Mazes of canyons and gullies stretch as far as the eye can see. The Sioux called this rough territory *mako sica,* or "bad lands." Today, it is the site of Badlands National Park.

The badlands is a beautiful example of the changing earth. Millions of years ago, this area was an inland sea. Over time, the sea dried out. To the west, the Black Hills pushed up from the ground. Streams carried huge amounts of sand, mud, and gravel there. Volcanic ash from the Rocky Mountains drifted east and covered the mud plain. Streams flowed over the land. They wore away much of this soft rock. Over time, wind and water carved the formations that appear today.

HOME OF THE SABERTOOTH: Badlands National Park is rich in fossils. Scientists have found evidence of a fascinating collection of prehistoric animals. The saber-toothed tiger and a three-toed horse once roamed there. Early ancestors of hogs, camels, and rhinoceroses have also been found. At other archaeological sites, traces of people have been discovered. Their tribes roamed this land 7,000 years ago.

VIEWS FROM THE WALL: A visit to this park is usually focused around the Badlands Wall. This 200-foot barrier runs for 100 miles and separates the prairie into two levels. To reach the wall, hikers follow several trails from Windows Overlook. Door Trail has a natural opening. As you step through it and see the badlands, it looks as if you have stepped onto the moon. Notch Trail and Windows Trail also provide fascinating views of gullies and canyons.

Visitors to the park see a changing world. Wind wears at the rock constantly. Rain is scarce, but sudden storms carry away soft rock from the wall. Parts of the Badlands look very different from the way they did only 50 years ago.

◀ *The park's 240,000 acres are divided by a wall of rock. From its lower plain, Badlands Wall is seen for miles. From the plain above it, the wall is invisible until you reach its edge.*

▲ *The term* **bad lands** *was first used to describe the South Dakota landscape. Similar rocky formations appear in other parts of the world.*

▲ *Pronghorn antelope graze on the grassy plains. Buffalo,* *mule deer, coyotes, bobcats, and bighorn sheep also live protected in the national park.*

Rocky Mountain

The Rocky Mountains separate the eastern and western sections of the United States. Their peaks form the Continental Divide. Water on the eastern slopes flows to the Atlantic Ocean. On the west, water reaches the Pacific. One beautiful section of the Colorado Rockies has been set aside as a national park.

Rocky Mountain National Park is America's highest park. Over 100 peaks in the park are 10,000 feet or taller. Highest of all is Longs Peak. Its summit is 14,255 feet tall.

TOO TOUGH FOR TREES: On the lower slopes of the park, hearty spruce, pine, and aspen trees thrive. As the trees grow up the slopes, they suddenly stop. About a third of the park's 265,000 acres is above the timberline. At these

◀ In the fall, the golden leaves of the aspen tree are a popular Rocky Mountain sight.

A series of beaver dams ▶ flood the lowland of Hidden Valley. Skiing and ice skating are popular winter pastimes in the valley.

▼ The surrounding landscape reflects in the waters of Nymph Lake. Shimmering lakes are common at Rocky Mountain. People fish in these lakes and in the park's mountain streams.

heights, trees cannot survive the harsh climate and short growing season. The tundra there is covered with meadows of tiny plants, short grass, and flowers. Mosses and lichen cling to the rocky surfaces.

Rocky Mountain is home to animals uniquely suited to the land. Mule deer and black bears live at lower elevations. Elk live higher up, as do golden eagles and hawks. Scattered on the park's steep cliffs are bighorn sheep. These agile creatures seem to defy gravity as they scamper along mountainsides. Bighorn sheep have become the symbol of this national park.

THE HIGHEST HIGHWAY: Rocky Mountain is a short drive from the Colorado cities of Denver and Boulder. Visitors often come to drive along Trail Ridge Road. From Estes Park at the east entrance, this road winds 44 miles through the park. Trail Ridge follows an old Native American path over the Continental Divide. It is the highest paved road in America. During one 10-mile stretch, it runs along a ridge 12,000 feet high.

More than 300 miles of hiking trails cover Rocky Mountain. At lower levels, visitors hike through tree-covered valleys and around clear mountain lakes. Mountain climbers go there, too. They are drawn by the challenge of the park's upper limits. One 8-mile trail rises 5,000 feet to the summit of Longs Peak.

Mesa Verde

Many national parks reveal evidence of human history. None can match the splendor of Mesa Verde. This park in the southwest corner of Colorado was the home of the Anasazi. The "ancient ones" built an elaborate city in the sandstone cliffs there.

The first tribes arrived at Mesa Verde 2,400 years ago. These early settlers planted corn and wove baskets. Over time, their civilization thrived. At first, people built houses on top of the cliffs. Around 1200, they began to construct intricate buildings in the cliff walls. These apartment buildings were several stories high. A typical structure had as many as 50 rooms.

THE ANCIENT ONES DISAPPEAR: In the years that followed, the Anasazi began to leave their cliff homes. By the year 1300, they were gone. Why they left, and where they went, remains a mystery. The abandoned cities lay hidden in the cliffs for nearly 600 years. They were discovered by cowboys in 1888.

Park rangers lead visitors through Mesa Verde's fragile ruins. Spruce Tree House is one of the best-preserved ruins. This building contains 114 rooms. The largest dwelling is 200-room Cliff Palace. This was the first building discovered and is still the most famous.

▲ *Cliff Palace is the largest community dwelling in Mesa Verde National Park. There are 4,000 prehistoric sights within the park's 52,000 acres.*

Cliff dwellings lay hidden ▶ *below the mesa top for centuries. When the Anasazi abandoned them, they left behind seed corn, pottery, jewelry, and weapons.*

▼ *This dramatic photograph outlines the plateau above the Anasazi cliff dwellings.*

Grand Teton

Just south of Yellowstone lies Grand Teton National Park. The Teton Mountains and the high valley, called Jackson Hole, are part of this beautiful park. Though much smaller than Yellowstone, Grand Teton has much to offer. It is rich in scenery, wildlife, and recreation.

The granite peaks of the Tetons are seen from every corner of the park. The highest peak, Grand Teton, rises 13,770 feet above sea level. Within the range, hikers find glacial lakes of clear blue water and rugged canyons.

A POPULAR SPOT: Jackson Hole is a valley 50 miles long. The Snake River flows from Jackson Lake and winds through the valley. Jackson Hole is a popular year-round resort. People come to fish, hunt, camp, and ski.

Wildlife thrives at Grand Teton. Moose, bison, and deer graze along the banks of the Snake River. Grizzly bears and bald eagles also live there. The park is the winter refuge for a herd of elk. The nearly extinct trumpeter swan is making a comeback in the park's sanctuary.

▲ *Grand Teton rises above the 310,000-acre national park named for it. Far below, a homesteader's log cabin has been carefully preserved.*

▼ *Six glacial lakes sit at the base of the Tetons. Waterfowl and fish flourish in the park's lakes and streams.*

Yellowstone

The first national park is still one of the most remarkable. Yellowstone is the largest parkland outside of Alaska. Its 2.2 million acres include the northwest corner of Wyoming and parts of Montana and Idaho.

The Rocky Mountain wilderness of Yellowstone is filled with wonders. Yellowstone Lake is the highest lake in America. The park has its own Grand Canyon, a deep orange-yellow gorge carved by the Yellowstone River. As the river races through the canyon, there are several waterfalls. One is twice as high as Niagara!

MUD POTS AND GEYSERS: Yellowstone's most famous marvels bubble up from the earth. The park includes over 10,000 geysers, hot springs, and simmering volcanoes of mud. More than half the geysers in the world are within the borders of the park. Old Faithful is Yellowstone's most famous geyser. Every 50 to 80 minutes, Old Faithful erupts. The geyser blasts hot water and steam as high as 200 feet into the air.

The explosive activity of Yellowstone is caused by volcanic activity below ground. In most parts of the world, the earth's crust is 20 miles thick. At Yellowstone, it is perhaps 2 miles thick. Molten magma boils below. As water seeps into the earth, it is heated by the magma below. It returns to the surface as steam.

▲ *Castle Geyser is thought to be Yellowstone's oldest geyser. Minerals from its hot water and steam have formed a cone around it that is 120 feet high.*

▼ *Clouds of steam rise from the geysers along the Firehole River. Among the geysers located near the river is Old Faithful.*

Water rising through ▶ *limestone formed Minerva Terrace, seen here in winter. As in cave formations, calcium carbonate deposits have created this dazzling effect.*

▼ *Morning Glory Pool is one of many thermal springs in the park. The rich, blue-green color is caused by algae living in the hot water.*

FOLLOWING THE LOOP: Visitors can spend days at Yellowstone and not see all its sights. One popular drive is along Grand Loop Road. This route circles 145 miles through the park. The road begins near Mammoth Hot Springs, site of thermal pools and eerie natural terraces of limestone. Grand Loop continues along the Firehole River through a series of geyser basins. Geyser Hill Nature Trail leads through the steamy, bubbling earth to Old Faithful.

Grand Loop Road crosses the Continental Divide and runs along the shore of Yellowstone Lake. As the road heads north, it offers spectacular views of Yellowstone's winding Grand Canyon.

More than 100 years ago, Yellowstone's startling beauty launched the national park movement. Today, it reminds its visitors of the importance of wilderness preservation.

Glacier

Glacier National Park is a giant, million-acre park in Montana. Joined with Waterton Park across the Canadian border, it forms the Waterton-Glacier International Peace Park.

The park is named for the natural force that carved this Rocky Mountain highland. Long ago, slow-moving rivers of ice sculpted deep valleys between the granite peaks. The remains of dozens of glaciers can still be seen frozen against the mountains.

Going-to-the-Sun Road is a 50-mile scenic highway through the park's center. The road crosses the Continental Divide and connects two of Glacier's more than 200 lakes.

HIKE TO THE ICE: Much of the park can only be enjoyed on foot. There are 700 miles of hiking trails. Some paths lead across alpine meadows. Others take visitors to the edge of two of the park's more than 50 glaciers. On some of the remote trails, hikers can go for days without seeing another person.

Plant and animal life is rich and varied in Glacier. The most famous resident is the endangered grizzly bear. About 600 grizzlies roam throughout the park.

▲ Glacier National Park features high granite mountains and glacial fields of ice. The largest glaciers in the park today cover about 300 acres.

◄ The clear blue water of Swiftcurrent Lake skirts around Grinnel Point. Gould Mountain can be seen in the background.

▼ Beautiful Kintla Lake in the North Fork Valley is near the Canadian border. It is one of the largest lakes in the park.

Arches

▲ The Windows is a famous sight in Arches National Park. It features a series of eight immense peepholes, including South Window seen here.

▼ Delicate Arch is the park's most famous landmark. Taller than a seven-story building, it sits at the edge of a red sandstone cliff.

Arches National Park is a giant rock garden in the Utah wilderness. The park contains over 950 natural stone arches. Strange rock towers and pinnacles are common sights. Other top-heavy formations seem to teeter in delicate balance.

WIND AND WATER SCULPTURE: The rock at Arches is sandstone. Millions of years of erosion have turned this soft rock into the fascinating shapes visitors see today. Landscape Arch, nearly the length of a football field, is the longest stone arch in the world. Balanced Arch, a 128-foot tower of rock, looks as if it is about to tumble to the ground any second. Scientists estimate it will stand for millions of years before erosion finally topples it.

Canyonlands

West of the Rocky Mountains sits the Colorado Plateau. This flat highland covers much of southern Utah. The deserted land is the site of more national parks than any other area in America.

Canyonlands National Park is southwest of Arches. The center of the park is the point where the Colorado River and Green River meet. The rivers have carved a deep canyon path. Flowing water, helped by wind, rain, and frost, has worn away rock, leaving formations on a grand scale.

DIVIDED BY RIVERS: The Green and Colorado rivers meet at the Confluence and flow south together. Their Y-shape splits the park into three regions. The northern section, called Island in the Sky, offers spectacular views. From Grand View Point, 2,500 square miles of canyon stretch to the horizon.

The western section, called Mazes, is some of the most secluded land in America. The most fascinating sight in Mazes is found in Horseshoe Canyon. Paintings on stone walls there, called pictographs, are believed to be 6,000 years old.

There are also pictographs in the Needles, the eastern section of the park. This is the most accessible part of Canyonlands. Needles features giant rock towers of red and white stone. The largest towers rise 400 feet from the canyon floor.

◀ *Canyonlands walls reveal evidence of human history. The Anasazi left traces of their work here as did artists from a much earlier time.*

▲ *Massive pillars are a common sight in the Needles section of Canyonlands. In the sunlight, they reveal more colorful layers of red and white rock.*

Capitol Reef

▲ *Salt Creek carves a steep, winding gorge as it flows through the eastern part of Canyonlands. The creek joins up with the Colorado River.*

Capitol Reef National Park is part of an immense 100-mile-long bulge in the earth, called the Waterpocket Fold. The land there rises 1,000 feet above the dry desert landscape.

CATTLE TRAILS AND COWBOYS: Capitol Reef sits on the Colorado Plateau between Canyonlands and Bryce Canyon National Park. Roads through the park follow trails that remind visitors of the West's colorful history. The scenic drive is built along a wagon path, called the Blue Dugway. Near this trail is Grand Wash, the canyon hideout of outlaw Butch Cassidy. Off an old cattle trail is Muley Twist Canyon. In pioneer days, mules had to wriggle to make it through the canyon's narrow passageway.

▲ *Misnamed, Capitol Reef is not a limestone reef at all. It is part of a huge buckle in the earth's crust, called the Waterpocket Fold.*

▼ *The walls of Capital Gorge feature thousands of pockets in the rock. These odd-looking formations are the result of wind and water erosion.*

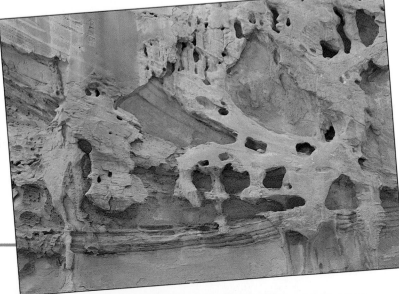

Zion

Only 125 miles north of the Grand Canyon, Zion National Park is unique. The canyons at most parks in southern Utah are viewed looking down from the rim. The pleasures of Zion are seen from the canyon floor.

The canyon floors at Zion are surprisingly lush. Visitors walk among willow and cottonwood trees. They stare up at huge sandstone rock formations. The Mormon settlers who arrived there gave the colossal formations inspiring names, like the Three Patriarchs, the Pulpit, and the Great White Throne.

A STEEP, NARROW GORGE: Zion Canyon, carved by the Virgin River, is the centerpiece of the park. Although its steep walls rise 3,000 feet to the rim, the canyon floor is never more than 20 feet wide. A short, six-mile scenic road ends at another popular sight—the Temple of Sinawava. The temple is a natural amphitheater. Two huge pillars, the Altar and the Pulpit, stand in the middle. From the temple, visitors follow three trails to other delights at the center of the park.

◄ *The Watchman stands tall above Zion Canyon. The rushing Virgin River continues to sculpt a path through the canyon gorge.*

Bryce Canyon

Bryce Canyon National Park is a fantasyland of stone. The iron-rich shale and sandstone have been carved into fantastic towers called hoodoos. The structures stand in dazzling rows, each one a unique, fanciful sculpture.

VIEW FROM THE TOP: The most magical vista in the 36,000-acre park is at Bryce Point. From this lookout, visitors see Bryce Amphitheater—a staggering series of red, white, and orange towers. Several trails lead down more than 8,000 feet into the amphitheater. Though only 4 miles wide, this part of the canyon floor has 21 miles of winding trails.

The towers and spires of Bryce Canyon are constantly changing. Erosion works quickly in the canyon. Its rim has moved back a foot since the park was founded in 1924.

◀ *Inspiration Point provides a fabulous view at Bryce Canyon. Spindle and tower formations have been given fanciful names such as Fairy Castle and the Cathedral.*

▼ *Paria View reveals the park's brilliant color in the twilight. Many canyon formations have been carved of red sandstone.*

▲ *Mammoth rock formations in Zion are 2,000 to 3,000 feet high. The Sentinel is seen here from the fertile canyon floor.*

Yosemite is one of the most famous and popular parklands in the United States. It was one of three national parks to follow Yellowstone's lead in 1890. Yosemite has a very important place in America's conservation movement. For more than 30 years, the fight to preserve and protect the park was led by naturalist John Muir.

Before Yellowstone was established, the wonders of northern California's Sierra Nevada mountains were well known. In 1864, a federal bill gave Yosemite Valley and the Mariposa Grove sequoia trees to California. These were to be kept as preserved state land. Today, the valley and grove are popular attractions in the 761,000-acre park.

GUARDING THE GORGE: Massive peaks of smooth, hard granite surround Yosemite Valley. At the east end of this seven-mile gorge, Half Dome rises to a height of 4,800 feet. At the western end of the valley, El Capitan is 3,600 feet high and even more massive. Scientists think El Capitan may be the largest block of granite in the world.

Water cascades from the heights of Yosemite. Waterfalls named Bridalveil, Ribbon, Vernal,

◀ Hidden in shadows is the steep vertical side of Yosemite's most famous peak. It is easy to see how the slice of rock called Half Dome got its name.

▲ Liberty Cap and Nevada Falls are among the sights in Yosemite. A hiking trail named in honor of naturalist John Muir leads past these and other wonders.

◀ The enormous granite peaks of El Capitan and the Cathedral face each other at one end of Yosemite Valley. The Merced River flows along the valley floor.

▼ Yosemite's largest sequoia, the Grizzly Giant, rises to the sky. After bristlecone pine trees, giant sequoias are the oldest living things on earth.

Nevada, and Iliiloutte are among the world's tallest. Yosemite Falls is the most famous one of all. The combined drop from its upper and lower portions is 2,425 feet. Yosemite is the tallest waterfall in North America and the third highest in the world.

A GROVE OF GIANTS: Yosemite has more than 1,200 of flowering plants and many kinds of trees. The most famous are the giant sequoias. The trees are among the oldest and largest living things on earth. Yosemite has three groves of sequoias. Among the 200 trees at Mariposa Grove is the Grizzly Giant—the fifth-largest tree in the world. This tree rises more than 200 feet toward the sky. It is more than 2,700 years old.

Yosemite is near the population centers of San Francisco, Fresno, and Sacramento. Every year, more than 2.5 million people come to see its wonders. The National Park Service struggles to make sure that overcrowding does not damage the natural beauty of Yosemite.

Sequoia and Kings Canyon

People who love national parks can double their pleasure at Sequoia and Kings Canyon. These two California parks sit side by side in the snow-covered Sierra Nevada mountains. The scenery is as big as it is beautiful.

Sequoia is the second oldest national park. It was founded in 1890, five days before Yosemite. It was established to protect groves of giant sequoias from being cut down by loggers. There are thousands of acres of sequoias within the park limits.

Kings Canyon National Park is a collection of granite mountains and rugged canyons. It includes the highest canyon wall in America. Kings Canyon rises from the Kings River over 8,000 feet to the top of Spanish Mountain. The park is an expansion of a small national park called General Grant. It became Kings Canyon in 1940. Since 1943, Sequoia and Kings Canyon have been managed as a single park.

A GIANT GENERAL: The biggest sequoias are as tall as 35-story buildings. The most famous one, named General Sherman, is the largest living thing on earth. General Sherman measures 275 feet to its treetop and 103 feet around its massive trunk. The trunk rises 130 feet before its first branch appears. This huge branch is larger than any tree found in the eastern United States! Several of the trees in Kings Canyon's Grant Grove are nearly as tall as General Sherman.

The mountains in the national park include the highest peaks of the Sierra Nevada. Among the peaks is Mount Whitney, the tallest mountain in the continental United States. Its snow-covered peak is 14,195 feet above sea level.

HIKING THE HIGH SIERRA: The alpine country of the Sierra Nevada is a hiker's paradise. The John Muir Trail is a high-mountain path that runs south from Yosemite 218 miles through Kings Canyon and Sequoia. Dozens of smaller trails branch into the park for views of canyons, glaciers, and alpine meadows.

▼ *Nearly four-fifths of the parkland is rugged high-mountain country. The gorge at Junction Ridge is typical of the Kings Canyon landscape.*

▼ *The fast-moving Kings River flows over boulders in Kings Canyon. Nearby Cedar Grove, with its ranger station, is a hub of activity in the park.*

▲ *Sequoia and Kings Canyon cover 864,000 acres in the Sierra Nevada. More than 300 miles of hiking trails in the park offer spectacular views.*

Tall sequoias stand on the ▶ forest floor. Sequoias are shorter than the redwoods of the California coast, but their trunks are much more massive.

Grand Canyon

The Grand Canyon is one of the great wonders of the natural world. This enormous and spectacular canyon was carved into the Arizona desert. Long known and admired, Grand Canyon National Park was established in 1919. In 1975, it was greatly expanded and now includes 1.2 million acres.

Most visitors approach the canyon from the south rim through flatland and pine forests. Suddenly, an enormous chasm more than a mile deep looms in front of them. Views from the wilder land on the north rim are also fantastic. On a clear day, the canyon stretches miles to the horizon. Even so, only a small portion of the park's 277 square miles can be seen from any overlook.

CARVED BY THE COLORADO: The Grand Canyon formed over hundreds of millions years. The final work was done by the powerful Colorado River. For at least 6 million years, it has flowed there, carving a deep path that became the canyon. Today, the river drops more than 2,000 feet on its 200-mile journey through the canyon.

The Grand Canyon's layers of rock reveal the

The Colorado River is a ▶ blue-green ribbon winding along the canyon floor. Although quiet here, the river is white-water rapids at other points.

◀ Yellow flowers on prickly pear cactus are a common Grand Canyon sight. The climate changes at different levels in the canyon.

▼ The Grand Canyon overlooks offer many spectacular views. At its widest points, the canyon is 18 miles from rim to rim.

◀ The setting sun brings out the rusty red color in the canyon's terraced walls. The layers of rock reveal billions of years of earth history.

▼ The desert plateau around the Grand Canyon has its own startling scenery. Huge eroded pillars, called buttes, are a majestic sight.

earth's history. The rock near the rim formed 250 million years ago. Below that lies older rock with fossils embedded in it. Older still is the hard, black stone on the canyon floor. This rock, dating back 2 billion years, is some of the oldest on earth.

MULES AND WHITE WATERS: Several trails lead into the canyon. The Bright Angel Trail winds for eight miles down the wall of the south rim. Many visitors make their way down this trail on muleback. The trail ends 4,600 feet below, where Bright Angel Creek flows into the Colorado. Some rustic cabins, which make up Phantom Ranch, are located there for people who want to spend a night on the canyon floor.

Another way to enter the Grand Canyon is on the Colorado River. Exciting raft trips begin at Glen Canyon Dam. During this long stretch of river, there are 160 sets of tumbling rapids. Visitors get a spectacular view and a thrilling ride.

Sequoias are more massive, but redwood trees are even taller. In many groves, these trees average more than 200 feet in height. Redwoods thrive in the foggy coastal land of northern California, site of Redwood National Park.

Tall Tree Grove is the center of the park. In this so-called cathedral grove, redwoods reach astounding heights. The tallest tree in the world is there. Tall Tree is nearly 368 feet high. The world's second- and third-tallest trees are nearby.

STRONG, VALUABLE WOOD: Redwoods are hearty trees. Their bark resists insects, fungi, and fire. The greatest danger to the trees is from humans, who cut them down for their highly valued hardwood. When it was established in 1968, Redwood National Park included 58,000 acres. Since then, it has nearly doubled in size. About 36,000 scarred acres are logged land now being left to return to its natural state. This slow process will take hundreds of years.

▼ *At sunset, fog rolls off the Pacific Ocean toward a redwood forest. The trees thrive in the warm, moist coastal air.*

Sunlight peeks through the ▶ *canopy of the redwood forest. It takes the trees about 400 years to reach their lofty heights.*

Painted Desert is a brilliantly colored badlands in northeast Arizona. Over 93,000 acres of this rough, beautiful land has been set aside in Petrified Forest National Park. The park is named for the rocky remains of an ancient forest scattered across the desert.

More than 200 million years ago, dinosaurs lived there. They roamed through tropical swampland. In the surrounding highlands were forests of conifer trees. Floods uprooted the trees and washed them into the lowland.

TURNED TO STONE: Buried by mud, sand, and volcanic ash, the trees underwent a slow change. Water seeping into the wood replaced its cells with hard stone. Over time, the soft land above wore away, revealing broken logs of stone. The logs vary in color depending upon their mineral content.

There are six separate "forests" of petrified wood in the park. Jasper Forest's many small fragments are scattered across the valley floor. Rainbow Forest has particularly colorful petrified wood. Several trunks there are over 100 feet long. Near Blue Mesa, petrified logs stands out in stark contrast to the soft-colored badlands.

▲ *Because oxygen did not reach them, petrified logs did not rot. Instead, mineral-rich water slowly turned them to stone.*

Each fragment of petrified ▶ *wood is a unique treasure.* ▼ *Gemlike crystal is at the heart of the log to the right. The specimen below is believed to be 160 million years old.*

Lassen Volcanic

Lassen Volcanic National Park sits at the southern end of the Cascade Mountains. The center of this park is towering Lassen Peak. The surrounding 106,000 acres form the smallest national park in California.

Lassen Peak, a long-dormant volcano, came to life in 1914. Over the next year, 150 minor eruptions occurred. Then, in May 1915, Lassen exploded, spewing out lava and sending a destructive river of mud to the valley below. The following year, the scorched land was set aside as a national park.

A SMOLDERING LANDSCAPE: The earth around Lassen still shows the effect of the eruption. Colorful names like Chaos Jumbles and Chaos Crag suggest a dangerous and spectacular world. At Bumpass Hell, hikers walk past bubbling mud pots and hissing geysers of sulfur. Another famous sight is Cinder Cone, a barren crater surrounded by cinder and ash. Farther from Lassen Peak, a forest of dwarf pines shows the slow healing process of nature at work.

▼ *Bumpass Hell is a mile-long valley of thermal activity. A walkway has been built through the steaming land here.*

▲ *Hat Creek runs through the foothills of Lassen National Park. Lassen Peak is an offshoot of a larger volcano called Mount Tehama. The Cascades are an active volcanic mountain range. Lassen was the last great eruption until the explosion of Mount St. Helens in 1980.*

Great Basin

▼ *Sunset highlights the misty hills of Great Basin. Trees grow in the foothills around Wheeler Peak where they are shielded from the worst desert climate.*

▲ *Lexington Arch is one of the spectacular sights hikers find in Great Basin National Park. The natural arch is 75 feet tall.*

Great Basin, established in 1986, is one of America's newest national parks. Its 77,000 rugged acres fan out around Wheeler Peak—one of the tallest mountains in Nevada.

Wheeler Peak is 13,063 feet tall. Its lower slopes are covered with pinon and juniper forests. Spruce, pine, and aspen cover the higher slopes. At its highest points, alpine meadows are covered with wildflowers.

ANCIENT PINE TREES: In the harsh climate at Wheeler's timberline live the park's greatest attractions. Forests of gnarled, twisted bristlecone pine trees cling to life through severe winters and long droughts. The hearty bristlecones are the world's oldest living trees. Some are 4,000 years old.

Another popular spot in the park is Lehman Cave. A mile and a half of trails in the cavern reveal an assortment of limestone formations. The most unusual are large, flat disks, called cave shields, which grow out of the ceiling.

Channel Islands

The Channel Islands is a 60-mile-long chain of islands off the coast of southern California. Five of the eight islands have been turned into a national park.

ABUNDANT MARINE LIFE: Wildlife is the great attraction at Channel Islands. Sea lions, elephant seals, sea otters, and fur seals flourish there. Seabirds, including the rare brown pelican, nest on the islands. Nearly 1,000 species of fish swim in the underwater kelp forests included in the park's 249,000 acres. This food source attracts gray whales during their migration along the Pacific coast.

Ancapa is the Channel Island closest to the mainland. Visitors come to hike the island trails for views of the rocky shore below. Traces of the Chumash people who once lived there can also be seen.

▼ *Interesting plants, including a treelike sunflower, grow on the Channel Islands. This grassy meadow is covered with flowering ice plants.*

A lighthouse stands on the ▶ cliffs of Ancapa. This Channel Island, 11 miles off the coast, is actually three separate islets covering 700 acres.

American Samoa

◀ *American Samoa's coastline has its share of fanciful rock formations. Camel Rock sits in the shallow waters near the island of Lail'i.*

▼ *Samoa receives more than 200 inches of rainfall every year. Exotic flowering plants like this beautiful plumeria bloom in this tropical paradise.*

Amerrican Samoa is the most far-flung parkland in the United States. The 8,800-acre park is located 2,500 miles south of Honolulu on the island of Samoa. This paradise contains volcanic mountains, rain forests, coral reefs, and magnificent white-sand beaches.

The island's rain forests are a rich habitat. Colorful tropical birds live there, as does the fruit-eating flying fox. This endangered animal is a huge bat with the wingspan of an eagle.

LIFE IN THE REEFS: Two coral reefs follow the coastline of American Samoa National Park. Octopus, sea snails, and hundreds of varieties of colorful fish live there. Rare hawksbills and green sea turtles live in the water off the reef. Another reef creature, the palolo worm, is considered a delicacy by the local population.

The Samoan people have inhabited the islands for 4,000 years. In 1988, to protect their land and their Polynesian culture, Samoan chiefs leased land to form America's newest national park.

▼ *Tutuila is Samoa's largest island. A natural harbor nearly divides the island in two. The village of Pago Pago, Samoa's capital city, is located here.*

Hawaii Volcanoes

The Hawaiian Islands were created by volcanoes pushing up mountains of lava from the Pacific Ocean floor. Hawaii is the newest and largest island in the chain. Two of Hawaii's five volcanoes are the main attractions at Hawaii Volcanoes National Park.

Mauna Loa reaches 13,677 feet above the Pacific Ocean. Its lava flow covers 2,000 square miles of the island. Kilauea is a side vent of the same mountain. This 4,000-foot volcano is still growing. Mauna Loa and Kilauea are two of the most active volcanoes on the planet.

VISITING THE VOLCANOES: In spite of their explosive activity, the volcanoes are relatively harmless. Eruptions there are predictable, and lava flows slowly. Visitors flock to the park to marvel at the earth's fury. When Kilauea is not erupting, people can stand at its edge and stare into its enormous crater.

The land around the volcanoes is a rich lava field. Although the black, rocky soil looks lifeless, it is surprisingly fertile. Plants quickly take root and grow unless they are wiped out by another sizzling-hot lava flow.

▼ *When rivers of hot lava flow, they destroy all plant life in their path. When lava cools and weathers, plants take root in this incredibly rich soil.*

Haleakala

On the Hawaiian Island of Maui, another volcano is preserved in Haleakala National Park. This quiet, or dormant, volcano has not erupted in 200 years.

Most of the park's 28,000 acres are contained within the huge crater at its summit. The crater is actually two high-mountain valleys joined by years of erosion. The crater floor is 3,000 feet below the rim. Two hiking trails lead into it.

Much of this land is a vast, desolate volcanic desert. Long-dormant cinder cones sit quietly inside the crater. At the eastern part of the crater, clouds roll over the edge, providing moisture. Exotic plants have taken root there. The rare Hawaiian goose, the nene, lives in this part of the crater.

AN OASIS NEAR THE OCEAN: A popular piece of parkland outside the crater is the Kipahulu Valley. The valley is a series of lush terraces linked by streams and cascading waterfalls. There is dense forest growth of clattering bamboo stalks and other trees. Mango and guava fruit are abundant, as are the colorful tropical birds that live there.

◀ *Kilauea's smoking crater, or caldera, is called Halemaumau. The crater covers six square miles. In one section is a huge, fiery pit of lava.*

▲ *The gray lava fields inside Haleakala Crater are a high-mountain desert. Foggy clouds rolling over its rim provide moisture for plant life.*

Olympic National Park is rich and diverse. The parkland's 922,000 acres include snow-capped mountains, rain forests, and rugged coastline. All these delights are a short drive from Seattle, Washington.

Mount Olympus is the highest peak of the Olympic Mountains. The jagged range features dozens of glaciers at its higher points and alpine meadows in its valleys and gorges. Heart O' the Hills Road offers sweeping, spectacular views to visitors who drive up this mountain road.

A NONTROPICAL JUNGLE: Parts of Olympic Park are the rainiest places in the United States. The parkland includes several rain forests, where plants equal the growth in tropical rain forests. Tall western cedar and Sitka spruce grow in the Hoh Rain Forest. Hoh contains over 70 kinds of mosses. They cover rocks on the forest floor and drape the limbs of tall trees.

Olympic includes 50 miles of Pacific coastline. Seals, sea lions, and whales live offshore. Marine birds nest on the rocky islands. Flocks of migrating birds are often seen in the flyway overhead.

The steep, rugged mountain peaks of North Cascades National Park are often compared to the Alps of Europe. This park in the state of Washington includes alpine meadows and high-mountain lakes. More than 300 glaciers continue to carve and shape the parkland.

The moist air from the Pacific reaches the western slopes of North Cascades and produces large amounts of rain and snow. Waterfalls and tumbling streams are common sights. Hanging icefalls and sheets of sloping ice are among the frozen formations in the park. In the warmer weather, the sound of cracking sheets of ice and rumbling avalanches is heard.

TWO PARKS IN ONE: The park's 684,000 acres are divided into two regions. Each is rough, beautiful wilderness. The northern section bordering Canada includes Mount Shuksan and other jagged peaks. The southern section is the location of the Stehekin River Valley. This deep canyon carved by glaciers is popular with hikers and backpackers.

◀ *Heavy rainfall has created lush forests in Olympic National Park. Hanging moss turns tree trunks and branches green. Ferns carpet the forest floor.*

▲ *Mount Shuksan is one of the dominant peaks in North Cascades National Park. Glaciers are a common sight near the craggy, granite peaks.*

▼ *Picture Lake sits at the bottom of a valley carved by glaciers. Mount Shuksan provides a beautiful wilderness backdrop.*

Mount Rainier

ount Rainier is one of the world's tallest volcanoes. The 14,410-foot mountain towers over surrounding Cascade peaks. Mount Rainier National Park is 235,000 acres of mountains, glaciers, lakes, and wilderness land.

Like huge fingers of ice, a system of 25 glaciers surrounds Rainier's volcanic peak. Emmons Glacier on the northeast flank is the most massive glacier south of Alaska. Six-mile Carbon Glacier is the longest. Flowering meadows and old forest sit just below the glaciers' end. On Rainier's lower slopes, lush plant life provides a home for bears, elk, and mountain lions.

HIKING AND CLIMBING: Rainier's Wonderland Trail is well named. This demanding, 93-mile hiking trail loops around the park and offers spectacular views of the mountain and its glaciers. Even more challenging is a climb to the Rainier summit. The park service conducts two-day climbs to the top. Inexperienced climbers spend a day learning to climb on ice and snow before beginning the ascent.

▲ *Wizard Island is a 760-foot-high mound of cinders in Crater Lake. Mount Scott can be seen rising in the distance.*

▼ *Viewed from Sunrise Point, Mount Rainier looks magical in the morning light. On a clear day, the mountain can be seen from more than 100 miles away.*

▼ *The water in Crater Lake is brilliant blue. There is no natural outlet for the water, so it is trapped in the lake.*

Crater Lake

Snow frequently covers ▶
Crater Lake. More than 50 feet of
snow falls every year. The snow
replaces water that evaporates
from the lake.

Crater Lake is the center of Oregon's only national park. The lake is actually the remains of a volcanic crater filled with water. The huge lake covers 26 square miles. At a depth of 2,000 feet, it is the deepest lake in America.

A COLLAPSING MOUNTAIN: Mount Mazama, site of Crater Lake, was once a 12,000-foot-high volcano. About 7,000 years ago, the mountain erupted for the last time. In its final explosion, the cone collapsed inward, creating an enormous crater. Over time, huge amounts of rain and melting snow filled the hole with water. Trees and plants took root in the rich volcanic soil surrounding the lake.

Visitors circle the lake as they make the 35-mile trip along Rim Drive. Boat rides are also a popular pastime. Among the sights are several islands sitting in the brilliant blue lake. Wizard Island is a cinder cone that formed at the time of the last eruption. Nearby hardened lava formed Phantom Ship Island.

Kobuk Valley

Alaska's national parks preserve some of the most spectacular wilderness land on earth. The eight parks there are enormous tracts of land. They cover over 41 million acres of wilderness—more land than all the other national parks combined.

Alaska's Kobuk River flows for 150 miles through a valley that is the heart of Kobuk Valley National Park. The slow-moving river is the main thoroughfare through the park's tundra and forest. Located above the Arctic Circle, Kobuk is one of the least-visited parklands in America. About 1,000 people come in a typical year.

SAHARA IN THE ARCTIC: The most startling sight in the park is Great Kobuk Sand Dunes. This expanse of sand covers 25 square miles on the east bank of the Kobuk River. Some of the dunes reach heights of 100 feet. This arctic desert is inching west and slowly taking over land now covered by a forest of spruce trees.

Kobuk's dunes are an ancient formation. They go back to a time when the continents of Asia and North America were connected by a land bridge at the Bering Straits. Prehistoric hunters crossed this bridge. The park is rich in archaeological treasures that date back 10,000 years. Traces of seven different cultures have been found in the parkland at Onion Portage.

Today, the Inuit tribe preserve their life-style in the park's borders. They hunt the great herds of caribou that pass through the park each summer.

▲ Some of the ancient sand dunes at Kobuk Valley National Park are 24,000 years old. The expanding desert grows about an inch every year.

The Kobuk River arrives from the Brooks Range and winds through the park's 1.7 million acres. In the Eskimo language, Kobuk means "great river." ▶

Gates of the Arctic

Gates of the Arctic National Park covers 8.5 million acres of Alaskan wilderness. This is America's northernmost parkland. Gates of the Arctic is located in the Arctic Circle.

HARSH WINTERS, SHORT SUMMERS: For much of the year, the climate in this part of the world is brutally cold. Temperatures often drop to −80°F. In its short summer, the sun stays in the sky all day and night. At this time of year, caribou come to feed on the moss and lichen that cover the tundra.

Naturalist Bob Marshall explored this land in the 1930s. He described it as the "gates of the Arctic" and led the fight for its preservation. Today, the land looks much as it did when he first saw it 60 years ago.

▼ *The bare Endicott Mountains rise above the Itkillik River. There are six wilderness rivers flowing through the park.*

Blazing colors brighten the ▶ *Arrigetch Valley. Gates of the Arctic's short growing season begins in mid-June.*

Glacier Bay

Glacier Bay is 3.2 million acres of wilderness on Alaska's southern coastline. The park contains more than 20 giant glaciers. Sixteen flow, like rivers of ice, toward the park's bays. As they do, huge chunks of ice break off the ends and fall into the water. This process, called calving, creates huge icebergs in Glacier Bay.

AN ICE-COVERED BAY: Glacier Bay is a park that is undergoing constant change. When explorer George Vancouver came 200 years ago, the entire bay was covered by a thick cap of ice. Since then, the glaciers have moved back 65 miles, carving the land as they recede. The ice has left behind a beautiful bay surrounded by mountains. Glacier Bay National Monument was established in 1925. Its area was expanded when it became a national park in 1980.

Scientists track the changes at Glacier Bay. They watch the ice move back and plants take root. Glaciers are receding as fast there as anywhere on the planet. The park provides clues about how the earth emerged from the last great Ice Age.

VIEWS FROM THE BAY: Visitors often explore the park by boat. They sail into the bay and see the

◀ A ship sails past a menacing hunk of ice floating in the chilly waters of Glacier Bay. The national park is best seen from the deck of a ship.

▼ The John Hopkins Glacier flows from the peaks of the Fairweather Mountains on the fringes of the park. The ice carves a track as it moves slowly forward.

◀ A cliff of ice on a rocky base rises above the water of Glacier Bay National Park. The bay is about 50 miles long and between 2.5 and 10 miles wide.

▼ As the glaciers move back, barren land is exposed. At the south end of the park, the land is now covered with a lush forest of spruce and hemlock trees.

action of the glaciers. Some glaciers move forward, cracking at the end and calving icebergs. Others recede, freeing up new ground for pioneer plants.

One of the most spectacular sights is Muir Glacier. The two-mile glacier has 265-foot-high ice cliffs that tower above the bay. This river of ice pushes forward 30 feet every day.

Glacier Bay National Park is rich in wildlife. Moose, wolves, mountain goats, black bears, and brown bears live in the park. Offshore, harbor seals and porpoises are common sights. Humpback whales come to feed on the vast reserves of krill in the coastal bays. Rare killer whales have also been sighted there.

Denali

Denali is Alaska's oldest park. In 1917, it was established as Mount McKinley National Park. The 20,320-foot peak, the highest in North America, towers over the mountains around it. In 1980, the park was expanded and its named changed. The ancient Athapaskan people called the mountain Denali, or "the high one."

Visitors come to Denali for the views of one of North America's greatest natural wonders. Snow-covered Mount McKinley is the source of many glaciers. Muldrow Glacier is a 35-mile sheet of ice that begins just below the summit. The glacier is an important route for climbers who wish to scale McKinley.

LIFE BELOW THE SLOPES: The mountain drops dramatically to tundra-covered valleys. Trees cannot grow above 3,000 feet in this harsh climate. When the snow melts, the tundra is covered with moss, lichen, and mats of blossoming wildflowers. Spruce, birch, and aspen trees grow in the park's lowest regions.

Denali's 6 million acres form one of America's largest wildlife preserves. Caribou thrive in its lichen-covered valleys. Wolves hunt in packs at the edge of the caribou herds. The rulers of this habitat are grizzly bears, which roam freely throughout the park.

Mount McKinley is often ▶ hidden in clouds. Best views are at dawn and dusk.

◀ Denali is located in central Alaska. Far below its granite peaks and tundra-covered slopes are trees and plants.

▲ A hike through the Valley of Ten Thousand Smokes leads to Katmai's crater lake. The effect of the 1912 eruption is seen.

Katmai

Katmai National Park is the site of Alaska's worst volcanic eruption of the century. In 1912, Mount Novarupta erupted, blasting ash 30,000 feet into the sky. The surrounding area was buried under hundreds of feet of steaming ash. The eruption caused the collapse of Mount Katmai's volcanic cone. Today, the cone is a blue-green crater lake.

The Valley of Ten Thousand Smokes is one of the park's attractions. After the 1912 eruption, thousands of vents in the ground sent smoke and steam spiraling into the sky. The landscape is no longer steaming, but it still shows the effects of that huge eruption.

WORLD'S LARGEST FISHERMEN?: Wildlife thrives in the park, which is famous for its brown bears—the largest meat eaters on land. About 750 brown bears roam throughout the park. The bears have lived in the region since ancient times. In midsummer, bear watching is at its peak near Brook Falls. From a viewing platform, visitors watch bears and their cubs fishing with their huge paws for salmon.

Green islets dot the waters of ▶ *Amelik Bay in Katmai National Park. The area is still shaken by powerful earthquakes.*

Lake Clark

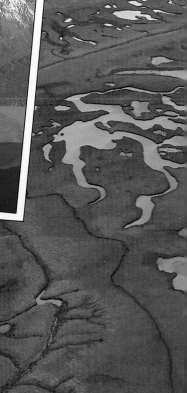

ake Clark National Park blends together many features of the Alaskan landscape. The high granite peaks of the Chigmit Mountains include two active volcanoes. The park also has scenic rivers, clear blue lakes, forests, and tundra. The 4-million-acre park is located 150 miles from the city of Anchorage.

ARRIVING BY AIR: Visitors take a one-hour flight from Anchorage to reach Lake Clark. Flying through a pass in the Chigmit range, they are treated to bird's-eye views of the park. After landing, many people explore the lake and its surrounding rivers in kayaks or other small boats.

Lake Clark is a varied wildlife preserve. Caribou, moose, black bears, and Dall sheep live in the park. Lake Clark itself is an important salmon spawning ground. In early summer, millions of fish swim up the Newhalen River to reach the lake. At times, the enormous number of salmon seems to turn the water red.

▲ *Lake Clark National Park can only be reached by air. Pilots often fly their small planes through passes in the 10,000-foot-high Chigmit Mountains.*

▼ *Lake Clark is 50 miles long and 5 miles wide. The lake's blue waters are fed by waterfalls and streams that pour out of the surrounding mountains.*

Kenai Fjords

◀ *The Kenai Peninsula continues to be shaped by powerful forces. These tidal flats were created by an earthquake that struck in 1964.*

▲ *The still waters at Moose Pass lead into the Kenai Mountains. This is a deceptively calm scene in a rugged, changing landscape.*

The rugged land of the Kenai Peninsula is the setting for Kenai Fjords National Park. At the center of the park is the Harding Ice Field. This enormous sheet of ice covers 700 square miles. Only the peaks of the Kenai Mountains reach above the ice, which is a mile thick in places. The mountaintops are called nunataks, which in Eskimo means "lonely peaks."

DEEP GLACIAL INLETS: Long ago, this entire region was covered with ice. The ice has receded, leaving behind a rugged coastline. Deep inlets, called fjords, slice into the mainland. Boats cruise into the fjords, providing views of steep walls of rock and snow-covered mountains. The fjords are home to harbor seals, sea otters, and humpback whales.

Kenai Fjords provides some of the best looks at Alaska's glaciers. More than 30 of them flow from the Harding Ice Field. A short trail leads to the edge of Exit Glacier. Visitors can picnic not far from this slowly receding river of ice.

Wrangell-St. Elias

Wrangell-St. Elias is a national park of grand proportions. There are more than 13 million acres of wilderness there, making it the United States' largest parkland by far. Wrangell-St. Elias is six time bigger than Yellowstone.

The Wrangell, St. Elias, and Chugach mountain ranges come together inside the park's borders. Nine of the United States tallest peaks are there. Mount Elias is the second highest at 18,008 feet. Guarded by these mountains are vast stretches of unexplored territory. There are valleys where people have never set foot and numerous mountains as yet unnamed.

AN ENORMOUS ICEFIELD: The Bagley Ice Field sits in the park's highland. Bagley is North America's largest icefield below the Arctic. More than 100 glaciers flow from it. One of the best known, the Malaspina Glacier, is larger than the state of Rhode Island.

Wrangell-St. Elias, a seldom-visited wilderness today, was once home to the Athapaskan people. The remains of their prehistoric settlements can still be seen inland. Along the coast, Yakutat is an old-style Tlingit fishing village.

◀ The Kennicott Glacier leads down from the mountain peaks in Wrangell-St. Elias. The glacier ends near the site of the old Kennicott copper mines.

▲ Although mountains dominate in the largest national park, there is a thriving coastline, too. Fishing is a major industry in the town of Wrangell.

▲ Fields of barley ripen during the short growing season in the Chitina River Valley. The snow-capped peaks of the Wrangell Mountains seem to float above the forest in the background.

◀ A huge glacier flows through Wrangell-St. Elias. Ice squeezing together forms a grooved pattern on the top of the glacier. These bumps are called pressure ridges.

The heart of the park is the Chitina River Valley. The Chitina is one of a dozen major rivers flowing out of the mountains. In the early 1900s, miners followed the rivers up to mineral-rich mountains in search of copper and gold.

VISITING THE MINES: A journey into Alaska's past begins at the point where the Chitina and Copper rivers meet. From there, a rough gravel road runs along the bank of the Copper River for 63 miles. A railroad once operated there, carrying ore from the copper mines upriver. At the end of the road, a hand-pulled cable car carries visitors across the Kennicott River. On the far side is the old mining town of McCarthy.

A few people still live in McCarthy, but none remain in nearby Kennicott. This ghost town was abandoned over 50 years ago. Still standing are a copper mill and mine—eerie reminders of a time when the parkland was valued for copper, gold, and other minerals.

Further Reading about Our National Parks

Boslough, John. *America's National Parks.* New York: Gallery Books, 1991.

Frome, Michael. *National Park Guide.* New York: Rand McNally and Company, 1985.

Winslow, Ellen. *America's National Parks.* New York: Gallery Books, 1991.

Picture Credits

Index